I·N·S·I·D·E
JAPAN

Ian James

Franklin Watts

London · New York · Sydney · Toronto

CONTENTS

© 1989 Franklin Watts
12a Golden Square
London W1

Published in the USA by
Franklin Watts Inc.
387 Park Avenue South
New York, N.Y. 10016

Franklin Watts Australia
14 Mars Road
Lane Cove
NSW 2066

Design: Edward Kinsey
Illustrations: Hayward Art Group

UK ISBN: 0 86313 834 9
US ISBN: 0-531-10760-4
Library of Congress Catalog
Card Number: 89-50384

Phototypeset by Lineage Ltd, Watford
Printed in Belgium

Additional Photographs:
C. Mccooey 5A, 8B, 10, 19, 20, 22A, 22B, 24A, 24B, 28, 29; Chris Fairclough 30C; Michael Holford 7, 8A; Geoff Howard 6, 12, 13, 16A, 16B, 17, 18A, 18B, 23; Hutchison 21; Japanese Information Centre 25, 26, 27; ZEFA 4, 5B, 9, 11A, 11B, 15

Front cover: Howard
Back cover: ZEFA
Frontispiece: Howard

The land

The island country of Japan is Asia's most developed country. The Japanese call it *Nippon*, or *Nihon*, which means *source of the Sun*. The four main islands, in order of size, are Honshu, Hokkaido, Kyushu and Shikoku. There are thousands of small islands, including The Ryukyu Islands, south of Kyushu, and the Bonin Islands, south of Tokyo.

The islands of Japan are the tops of a long mountain range which rises from the floor of ocean. This range lies on an unstable part of the Earth's crust. Volcanic activity and earthquakes are common. The highest mountain, Mount Fuji, or Fujiyama, is a volcano. Its peak is 3,776 m (12,388 ft) above sea level.

Below: **The northeast coast of Hokkaido has many beautiful beaches and wave-worn rock formations.**

Above: **Flat land is scarce in Japan. Every bit of level land is farmed.**

Left: **Mount Fuji, Japan's highest peak, is a volcano; it last erupted in 1707.**

Forested mountains and hills cover seven-tenths of Japan and there is much beautiful scenery. Most people live in the crowded coastal lowlands, the largest of which is the Kanto Plain around the capital city Tokyo.

The climate varies from south to north. Kyushu and Shikoku are warmed by the tropical Japan Current and they have hot summers and mild winters. Southern Honshu has warm summers and mild winters. The winters in northern Honshu and Hokkaido are cold and snowy. The climate in the north is affected by the cold Oyashio Current which originates in the icy north. Most of Japan has abundant rainfall.

Above: **Monsoon winds from the northwest bring cold air and snow to Hokkaido in winter.**

The people and their history

The first inhabitants of Japan were probably the Ainu, who now form a minority of less than 20,000 people living in Hokkaido. However, the ancestors of most modern Japanese people had probably settled there about 2,200 years ago.

In 1603, the Tokugawa family took control of a newly united Japan and cut Japan's ties with the outside world. This policy ended in 1853 when US Commodore Matthew Perry arrived with a fleet of ships and made Japan open its ports to foreign trade. To prevent Japan becoming a colony, the Japanese worked hard to modernize and industrialize their country. Their power was tested in 1894-5, when Japan defeated China, and in 1904-5, when Japan defeated Russia.

Below: **In early times, rival families hired bands of samurai warriors when they fought for control of the government. This painting dates from the 18th century.**

Above: **A naval battle in the Russo-Japanese War (1904-1905), when Japan amazed the world with its victories.**

Left: **The Americans dropped an atomic bomb on Hiroshima. It exploded directly above the Hall in this picture and caused great destruction all around it.**

On December 7, 1941, Japan entered World War II when it attacked the American base at Pearl Harbor. During the war, Japan occupied many countries in eastern Asia.

Japan surrendered in 1945 after atomic bombs were dropped on the cities of Hiroshima on August 6 and Nagasaki on August 9. American troops occupied Japan until 1952. The Emperor, who had been regarded as a god, remained Head of State. But he publicly gave up his status as a god and became a ceremonial monarch. Japan is actually ruled by an elected Diet (parliament), the prime minister (usually the leader of the main party in the Diet), and the cabinet.

Above: **The Imperial Palace is the home of the Emperor, Japan's Head of State.**

9

Towns and cities

Above: **A mountain farm in central Honshu. Many farming people have part-time jobs in nearby towns.**

Between 1870 and 1970, Japan's population tripled in number. Today, with more than 120 million people, it is the world's seventh most populous nation. But the yearly rate at which the population is growing has recently slowed down to 0.8 per cent.

The large increase in the national population has resulted in a fast expansion of cities and towns, where most of Japan's new industries are situated. For example, the city of Yokohama, Japan's second largest urban area after Tokyo, was a tiny fishing village when Commodore Perry arrived in Japan in 1853. Today, only 24 per cent of the people live in rural areas, and many of them have part-time jobs in factories and offices in nearby towns.

Left: **The city of Chiba, about 35 km (22 miles) east of Tokyo, has large housing estates built on land reclaimed from Tokyo Bay.**

Below: **Sapporo is the largest city on the island of Hokkaido.**

Apart from Tokyo, the main cities are Yokohama, Osaka and Nagoya. Yokohama is Japan's third most important port (after Chiba and Kobe) and it is also a major commercial and industrial city. It has been rebuilt twice: first after a severe earthquake in 1923, and second after it was bombed in 1945. Osaka is a "castle town" – that is, it grew up around a castle from which samurai warriors ruled the area. Nagoya is another castle town, which is now a major industrial city.

Japan's fifth largest city, Sapporo, is on the island of Hokkaido. It is an attractive, modern city, with a well laid out network of streets. The sixth largest city, Kyoto, was Japan's capital from 794 to 1868. It has many old buildings which recall its historic past.

Below: **Many cities contain graceful old buildings. The temple of Toudajai at Nara, on south Honshu, contains the world's largest bronze statue of Buddha.**

Above: **Tall modern buildings give Tokyo the appearance of a Western city.**

Sapporo

Sendai

Tokyo

Yokohama

Nagoya

Hiroshima

Kobe

Kyoto

Nagasaki

Above: **The map shows some of the major cities and routes in Japan.**

In 1868, Kyoto was replaced as capital by the city of Edo, which was renamed Tokyo, a word meaning eastern capital. Tokyo stands on Tokyo Bay. It was badly damaged by an earthquake in 1923 and by bombing in 1945. Most of Tokyo now looks like a Western city, but it retains some beautiful places.

Among the city's highlights are the Imperial Palace and its attractive gardens, and Ueno Park, which has magnificent displays of cherry blossoms in spring. The many places of worship include the impressive Meiji Shrine, dedicated to the Emperor Mutsuhito, who made Tokyo the capital city. Other landmarks include the Tokyo Tower (a tall TV and radio mast), the National Diet Building and the Ginza, a fashionable shopping street.

Below: **The map shows some of Tokyo's landmarks.**

1 Sunshine and City Prince Hotel
2 Rikugien Gardens
3 Ueno Park
4 Asakusa Kannon
5 Tokyo Hilton International
6 Budokan Hall
7 Skinjuku Gyoen Garden
8 Akosaka Palace
9 Imperial Palace
10 National Diet
11 Meiji Shrine
12 Yoyogi Sports Centre
13 Tokyo Tower
14 Central Wholesale Market
15 Kabukiza Theatre

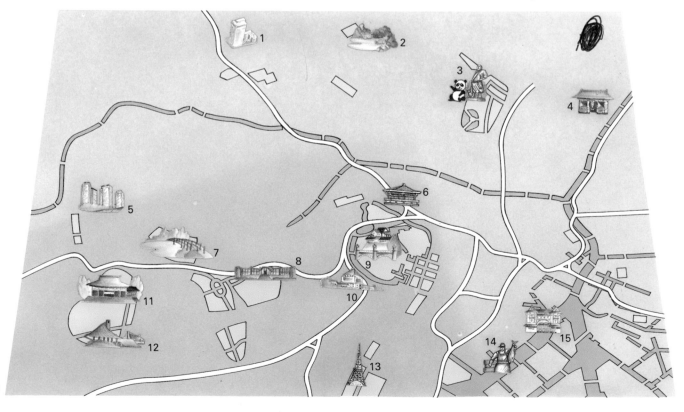

Family life

Forty years ago, most people lived in small wooden houses with thatched or tiled roofs. The rooms were separated by paper screens, which could be moved to change the shape and size of the rooms. Today, many city people live in modern apartments.

Households once contained members of three generations. But the average size of households has dropped to three. Men once dominated the home, but recently women have gained more freedom and an increasing number now have jobs. Men once spent most of their time at work, but they now have more leisure time with their families. Hard work remains a virtue. Many children go to evening "cramming" schools to make sure they pass their examinations.

Left: **A patchwork of fields surrounds most villages. The rice fields are flooded at the start of the growing season.**

Left: **Many city people now live in modern apartments.**

Below: **Computer games are popular activities in the home.**

Food

Rice is Japan's most important traditional food, though many people now eat bread instead of rice at some meals, such as breakfast. Fish, Japan's main source of animal protein, and vegetables are eaten with rice. A popular meal, called *sushi*, consists of small balls of vinegared rice topped by raw fish, shellfish or pickle. Soya beans (soybeans) are also rich in proteins and they are used in many dishes, including sauces and soups. Meat and dairy products were unusual 40 years ago, but they are now eaten by many young people.

Famous dishes include *sukiyaki* (sliced beef cooked with vegetables) and *tempura* (seafood, seaweed or vegetables deep-fried in batter). Green tea, without milk or sugar, is the most popular beverage.

Below: **Japan has some supermarkets, but many people prefer to shop at small stores.**

Above: **Popular dishes include** *sushi* **(raw fish on balls of vinegared rice), soy sauce, pickled radish and miso soup (made from soya beans).**

Below: **The Japanese use chopsticks to eat at home and in restaurants.**

Sports and pastimes

Sumo, Japan's leading spectator sport, is an ancient form of wrestling. The aim of each contestant is to force his opponent to touch a straw-rope circle with any part of his body except the soles of his feet, or to force the opponent out of the ring. Another sport, better-known in the West, is *judo*, a form of unarmed combat. *Kendo* is a form of fencing using bamboo swords, while *karate*, which came from China, is a form of unarmed combat using the hands, elbows, knees or feet.

The leading Western sport is baseball, which was introduced by American missionaries. Many businessmen enjoy golf. But land is scarce and only the wealthy can afford to join one of the golf clubs. Most people make do with playing at golf driving ranges.

Below: **The rules of *sumo* are much simpler than those of Western wrestling.**

Japan's beautiful mountains attract many climbers and walkers, and skiing is popular in winter. Less energetic pastimes include *ikebana*, or *kado*, the art of flower arrangement, the *chanoyu*, or tea ceremony, and *origami*, the art of paper folding.

The leading festival in Japan is New Year's Day, when people wear kimonos (traditional robes fastened with sashes), attend religious shrines and visit their friends and relatives. Other festivals include the Emperor's Birthday, Children's Day and Respect for the Aged Day.

Most Japanese spend their annual vacation in Japan, but foreign travel is increasingly popular. In 1986, 5.5 million Japanese went abroad.

Above: **Young women, called geisha, conduct a tea ceremony. Geisha are trained in the art of entertaining guests with conversation, music and dance.**

The arts

Calligraphy (the art of beautiful handwriting) and painting are two of Japan's leading arts. Religion has greatly influenced architecture and sculpture. Many Buddhist temples contain superb statues of Buddha and demons.

Traditional music remains popular but many people also enjoy Western symphonic music. Forms of Japanese drama include *Noh* plays in which the actors are masked; *Bunraku*, or puppet plays; and *Kabuki*, melodramas in which all the actors are men. Several Japanese film-makers are known internationally. They include Akira Kurosawa (1910-   ), who made many impressive movies, such as *The Seven Samurai* (1954). One of the best known works of Japanese literature is *The Tale of Genji*, written in the 11th century.

Below: **The actors in Kabuki plays wear elaborate costumes.**

Above: **This huge bronze statue of the Buddha is at Kamakura, a small town south of Tokyo.**

Left: **The face of a Kabuki character appears on a kite, that is flown at the New Year's Festival.**

Farming

Farmland covers less than 15 percent of the land, while forests cover nearly 70 percent. Most farms are small, but farmers use fertilizers and farm machinery designed for small plots and so yields are high. Rice, the leading crop, is grown on nearly half of the farmland. Other crops include barley, fruit and vegetables, beans and wheat.

Nearly 5 million cattle, 11 million pigs and 337 million chickens are reared for meat. But fish remain the main source of animal protein. Japan is the world's leading fishing nation, accounting for about a seventh of the world's total catch. Farming, fishing and forestry employ 11 percent of the workforce. But Japan produces only about 70 percent of the food it needs. The rest is imported.

Below: **Special machines designed for small fields have helped Japanese farmers to raise their crop production.**

Above: **Rice is hung up to dry before threshing.**

Left: **Frozen tuna fish are auctioned in Tokyo.**

Industry

Japan has a wide variety of minerals, but most of the deposits are small. As a result, Japan has to import most of the materials, including coal, oil and metals, which it needs for its factories. Yet through hard work, efficiency and great technical skill, the Japanese have made their country the world's third leading industrial power after the United States and the Soviet Union. Industry now employs 34 percent of the workforce and it accounts for 40 percent of the total value of all the goods and services produced in Japan.

Japan is the world's second largest producer of steel after the Soviet Union, and it leads the world in building ships, cars, commercial vehicles and motorcycles.

Left: **The electronics industry employs a large number of women.**

Left: Japan has an extensive transportation network, though new roads must be built to cope with the rapidly increasing number of cars.

	Fishing port		Mining
	Mandarin oranges		Industry
	Grapes and other fruit		Ship-building
	Rice		Cattle

Above: **The map shows some of the economic activities in Japan.**

Many Japanese industries are based on electronics. Japan leads the world in making television sets and it also produces radios, video cameras and recorders, computers, hi-fi equipment and electronic calculators. It is also known for its cameras and such appliances as washing machines and refrigerators. The chemical and textile industries, including the manufacture of silk, are also important.

Japan is the world's third most important trading nation. Manufactures are the main exports, and raw materials, fuels and food are the chief imports. Japan's leading customer is the United States, followed by Southeast Asia.

Left: **Yokohama is now one of Japan's largest ports.**

Looking to the future

Defeated in 1945, with its economy in ruins, Japan has become one of the world's most prosperous countries. Wages are high, but housing and food are expensive. But most people live comfortably. The cities contain some poor areas, but there are few slums.

Japan's economy continues to grow and the country invests heavily in research into new products and more efficient industrial methods. The rate of unemployment is one of the world's lowest and Japan has a more reliable, more loyal and better educated workforce than many Western industrial countries. Competition is strong from schooldays onward and failure sometimes leads to suicide.

Above: **the late emperor, Hirohito, the new emperor, Akihito and their wives greet New Year well-wishers in 1985.**

Despite its great economic importance, Japan is not a military power. Under its Constitution, which came into effect in 1947, its military forces exist only for defensive purposes.

Many other countries would like to see Japan play a greater role in world affairs. Japan has long been hampered by its language, which is not spoken in any other nation. This means that many people are isolated from outside influences. But this is slowly changing as more Japanese travel and work abroad. Japan has also greatly increased its aid to developing countries and it plans to increase the number of foreign students in Japan from 15,000 to 100,000 by the year 2000. At every level, contacts between the Japanese and outsiders are steadily increasing.

Below: **Education is free and compulsory for children between 6 and 15. Many children go on to high schools and universities.**

Facts about Japan

Area:
377,708 sq km
(145,834 sq miles)

Population:
122,124,000 (1987)

Capital:
Tokyo

Largest cities:
Tokyo (pop 8,354,000)
Yokohama (2,993,000)
Osaka (2,636,000)
Nagoya (2,116,000)
Sapporo (1,543,000)
Kyoto (1,479,000)
Kobe (1,411,000)

Official language:
Japanese

Religion:
Shintoism, Buddhism,
Christianity

Main exports:
Manufactured goods,
including machinery,
motor vehicles and
electronics

Unit of currency:
Yen

Japan compared with other countries

Japan 323 per sq km

Britain 232 per sq km

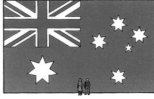

USA 26 per sq km

Australia 2 per sq km

Above: **How many people?
Japan is more densely
populated than Britain.**

Below: **How large?
Japan is a little larger than
Britain.**

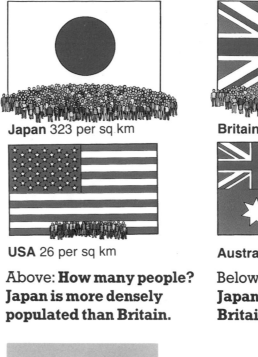

USA　　　　　　　Australia　　　　　Japan　　UK

Below: **Some Japanese
money and stamps.**

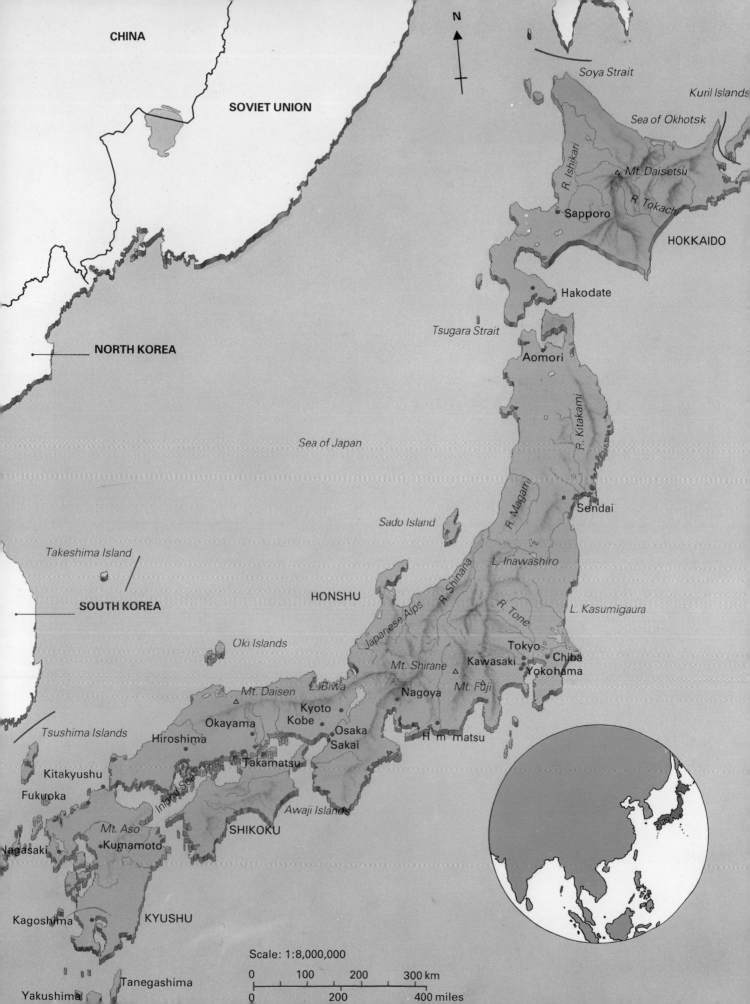

CHINA

SOVIET UNION

N

Soya Strait

Kuril Islands

Sea of Okhotsk

R. Ishikari

△ *Mt. Daisetsu*

R. Tokachi

● Sapporo

HOKKAIDO

Hakodate

Tsugara Strait

Aomori

R. Kitakami

NORTH KOREA

Sea of Japan

R. Mogami

Sendai

Sado Island

L. Inawashiro

Takeshima Island

R. Shinana

L. Kasumigaura

HONSHU

R. Tone

SOUTH KOREA

Japanese Alps

Tokyo ●

Oki Islands

Mt. Shirane

Kawasaki

Chiba

△

Yokohama

Mt. Daisen

L. Biwa

Nagoya

Mt. Fuji

△

Kyoto ●

Okayama

Kobe

Tsushima Islands

Hiroshima

Osaka

H m matsu

Sakai

Takamatsu

Kitakyushu

Inland Sea

Fukuoka

Awaji Islands

SHIKOKU

Mt. Aso

Nagasaki

Kumamoto

KYUSHU

Kagoshima

Scale: 1:8,000,000

0   100   200   300 km

0   200   400 miles

Tanegashima

Yakushima

Index

PRINTED IN BELGIUM BY

proost
INTERNATIONAL BOOK PRODUCTION

DATE DUE		
JAN 0 3 1993		APR 1 1 2002
	NOV 1 0 '97	
MAY 1 3 1994	DEC 1 0 '97	
AUG. 0 1 1994	MAR 2 2 99	MAY 1 8 2005
JAN. 2 4 1995		
MAY 6		FEB 1 4 2008
OCT 2 4	MAY 1 7 '99	
	OCT 2 6 00	
AUG 2 6		
SEP 1 9 '96		OCT 0 7 2001